MW01097731

Big Book of Beginner's Piano Classics

Volume Two

57 Favorite Pieces in Easy Piano Arrangements

David Dutkanicz

DOVER PUBLICATIONS, INC.
Mineola, New York

All songs available as downloadable MP3s!

Go to: http://www.doverpublications.com/0486812669
to access these files.

Bibliographical Note

Big Book of Beginner's Piano Classics Volume Two is a new compilation of works by David Dutkanicz, which have been reprinted from authoritative editions. The author has selected and arranged the works and provided the introductory material, as well as an Introduction and Notes on Duets, especially for this Dover edition.

International Standard Book Number
ISBN-13: 978-0-486-81266-3
ISBN-10: 0-486-81266-9

Manufactured in the United States by LSC Communications
81266901 2017
www.doverpublications.com

CONTENTS

DUETS

Works are arranged in alphabetical order by composer.

However, some works have been placed in such a way that it is easier to facilitate page turns.

INTRODUCTION

The original *Big Book of Beginner's Piano Classics* has become a popular staple for piano students and enthusiasts alike. This next volume continues the mission of the first: to bring the joys of classical music to beginners of all ages and stages. These works have been carefully chosen and span repertoire from the seventeenth through the twentieth centuries. As an added bonus, five duets have been selected for this edition. Fingerings are once again provided as suggestions; however, each performer is encouraged to customize them to their preference. Phrasing and pedaling are also left open to be filled in as progress is made and the eyes become more comfortable reading music. It is our hope that this newest volume continues to entertain as it helps pianists to develop their fingers and ears.

DUETS

A new feature introduced in this volume is duets. For those new to playing piano duets: Piano I sits to the right, and Piano II to the left. This is also how the music appears in the book: Piano I music is on the right-hand side of the book, and Piano II to the left. When practicing with another, you can use the measure numbers in the music to keep track of where you are in the music.

Note to Teachers: Duets are one of the best ways to demonstrate musicality to students and to teach key principles. Both Piano I and II parts have something to offer. Each duet can also help focus on a specific skill. The following are suggested:

- *Chopsticks:* intro to duets, playing in rhythmic unison with another
- *Chorale No. 96:* four-voice playing, interaction of individual lines
- *Für Elise:* melody versus accompaniment, counting rests
- *Great Gates of Kiev:* confidence playing *forte* in the lower register (Piano II)
- *Symphony No. 25:* syncopation

Traditional—*Chopsticks*

This very popular piano staple was first published in 1877 and was originally known as the "Chop Waltz." The composer attributed to the first edition was Arthur de Lulli. However, it has been discovered that this was a pseudonym for Euphemia Allen, whose brother-in-law was a music publisher. In this arrangement, Piano I and II play in unison, separated by two octaves. This is a chance to practice playing evenly and in time with another performer.

J. S. Bach—*Chorale No. 96*

J. S. Bach set quite a number of hymns as four-voice chorales. This is No. 96, which uses a frequently set text, "Jesu, Meine Freude" ("Jesus, my Joy"). The bottom two voices are in Piano II, and the top in Piano I. Play evenly and reverently, bringing out individual melodic voices.

Ludwig van Beethoven—*Für Elise*

Für Elise is one of Beethoven's most famous works, and one of the most well-known in all of music. This arrangement gives the melody to Piano I, with the original accompaniment divided between the two hands of Piano II. It is very important to count rests and be confident of your entry.

Modest Moussorgsky—*Great Gates of Kiev*

This powerful work is the closing movement of *Pictures at an Exhibition*. The texture is chorale-like and should be played with a full and majestic sound. Also, note the extra power of the melody when it is played in octaves. Both performers should play as one.

W. A. Mozart—*Symphony No. 25*

This is one of Mozart's most performed symphonies, and it contains a very energetic opening. The notes are accented on off beats, an effect known as *syncopation.* The opening, played in rhythmic unison, is a perfect way to practice and teach syncopation.

Big Book of Beginner's Piano Classics

Volume Two

Carl Philipp Emanuel Bach

(Germany, 1714–1788)

Pastorale

Pastorales are musical works meant to evoke feelings of calm and peace. C. P. E. Bach (son of Johann Sebastian) uses a musical device known as parallel thirds to create this atmosphere. As the melody moves, it carries a harmony which is a third above.

Johann Sebastian Bach

(Germany, 1685–1750)

PRELUDE NO. 3

(from *The Well-Tempered Clavier,* Book I)

J. S. Bach is regarded as one of history's finest composers and a master of counterpoint. Counterpoint is the interplay of individual voices within a work, creating an overall unifying effect. Imitation is a contrapuntal device where voices echo what came before them. In this Prelude, the left hand imitates what was previously played by the right.

Béla Bartók

(Hungary, 1881–1945)

YUGOSLAVIAN MELODY

(Mikrokosmos I, No. 40)

In addition to being a composer, Bartók was an avid musicologist who studied the music of various cultures. Many of these found their ways into his compositions, such as this one. The static repetition in the left hand is known as a drone. You can set it on "auto pilot" and focus on making the right-hand melody sing and dance.

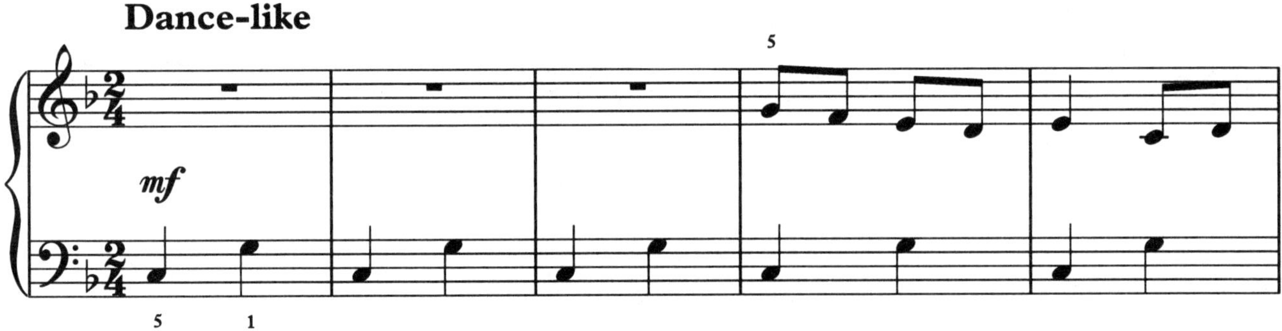

14
1

18
3

22
5

26

Béla Bartók

(Hungary, 1881–1945)

Imitation and Inversion

(Mikrokosmos I, No. 23)

Mikrokosmos is a collection of 153 piano pieces intended primarily for instructional purposes. This study trains right and left hands to imitate one another. Notice that the composer alternates which goes first, creating a different sound both times. It's challenging for your fingers and ears, but this will help train your hands to be independent of one another.

Ferdinand Beyer

(Germany, 1803–1863)

DER NIBELUNGEN HORT

(Op. 98, No. 2)

This work is the second of two pieces from 2 Etudes Mélodiques. It recalls the old German *Nibelungen* tales and its horde of treasures—including the magical ring central to Wagner's *Ring Cycle* of operas. Take note of the thirds in the left hand.

Andante

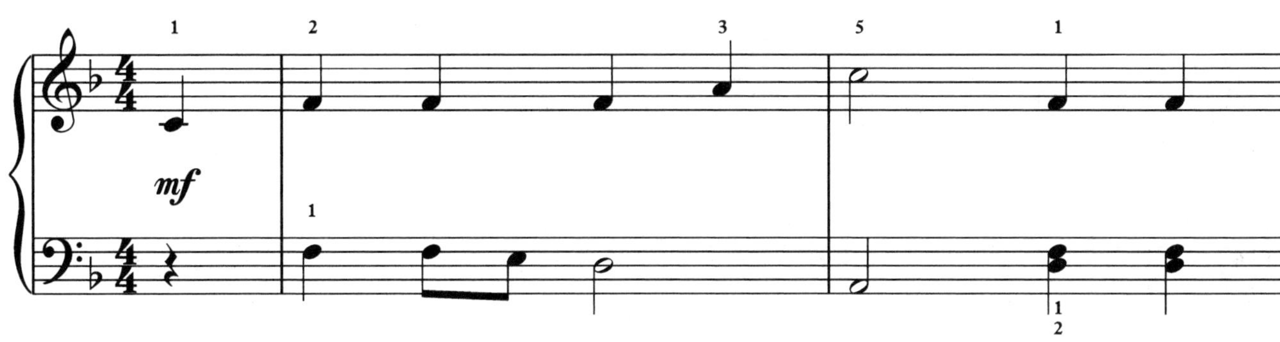

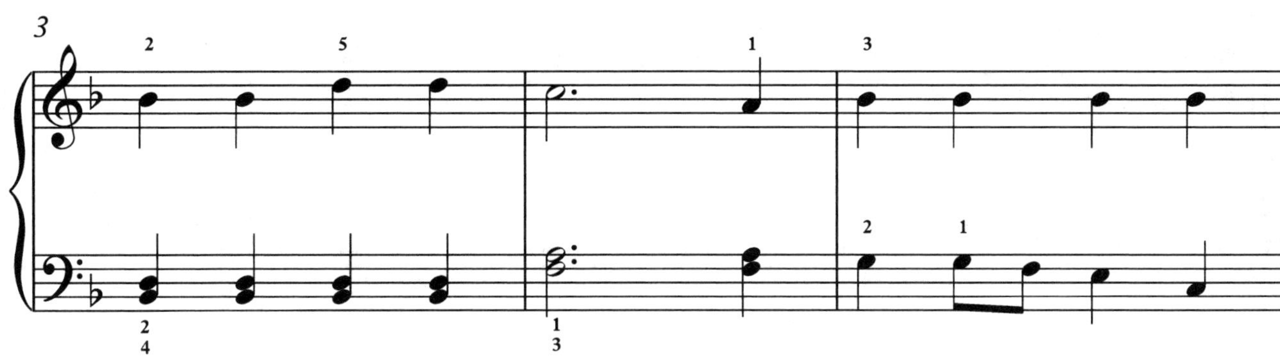

Ferdinand Beyer

(Germany, 1803–1863)

Mon Étoile

(Op. 116)

Mon étoile means "my star" in French and is also popular in a Polish version, "Gwiazdka." You will find that the song does have moments of shining and brightening. Note at measure 9 how the mood changes. By contrasting minor and major chords, the music creates shades of light and dark.

With emotion

13

17

21

Ferdinand Beyer

(Germany, 1803–1863)

Evening Song

(Op. 101, No. 58)

Ferdinand Beyer is best known today for his instructional *Beginning Piano School,* Op. 101. It is a delightful collection of short works designed to help students progress musically. When playing this work, use a hushed sound and a calm tempo.

Ferdinand Beyer

(Germany, 1803–1863)

Swiss Melody

(Op. 101, No. 85)

This charming tune uses a yodel-like melody in the right hand to evoke the Swiss Alps. The opening passage will require the thumb to cross underneath the forefinger to reach the next note. With the thumb on G, it will be easier to reach the E above. Isolate this motion (E-F-G) when practicing, beginning slowly and smoothly until it is up to tempo.

Moderato

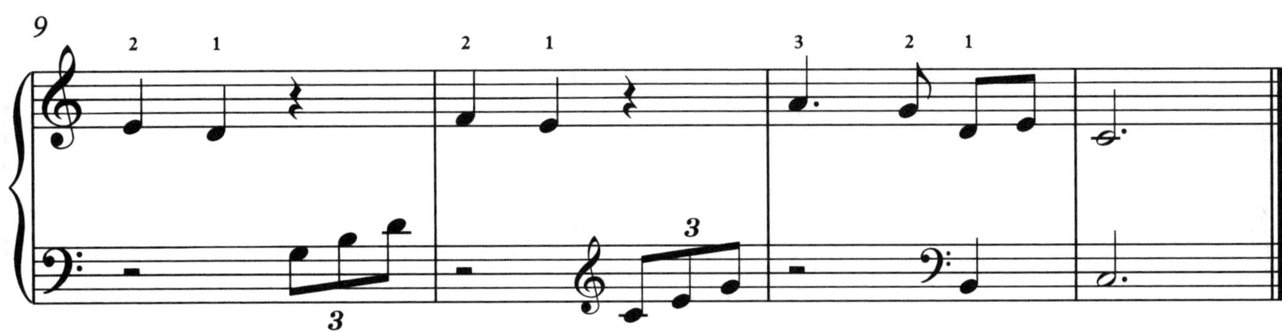

Muzio Clementi

(Italy, 1752–1832)

Waltz

Muzio Clementi was born in Italy, but spent most of his life in London. He was quite prolific, and his music has a special place in keyboard repertoire. In addition, he was also a piano manufacturer. This was at a time when it was still new and gaining acceptance to replace older keyboard instruments such as the harpsichord and clavichord.

François Couperin

(France, 1668–1733)

THE REAPERS

("Les Moissonneurs")

This work is taken from the famous tome *Livre de Pièces de Clavecin (Book of Pieces for the Harpsichord)*. The mood is of the harvest, and the parallel thirds that appear in the left hand are evocative of a *pastorale*. Play it lightly and at a moving tempo.

César Cui

(Russia, 1835–1918)

Causerie

(Op. 40, No. 6)

César Cui was a member of the Mighty Five of Russian composers, alongside Balakirev, Borodin, Moussorgsky, and Rimsky-Korsakoff. This lovely piece, published in 1887, is from a collection of nine entitled À Argenteau. When practicing, divide the work into 2 and 4 measure sections, and focus on the leaps in the melody.

13
1
1
1
2
3
5
2

17
1
1
4
2
2
mp
2

21
1
1
4

William Duncombe

(England, *ca.* 1736–1819)

SONATINA

William Duncombe was an English composer who was also a church organist in Kensington. He was active during the years of the Classical period, and his works reflect the transition from the English Baroque. When playing, be mindful of the triplets and play them evenly. If the tempo is rushed, the triplets will not be played properly.

César Franck

(Belgium, 1822–1890)

Panis Angelicus

(from *Mass*, Op 12)

Panis Angelicus is Latin for "Bread of the Angels." It is part of César Franck's *Mass*, Op. 12, and has been recorded by a wide variety of artists including Luciano Pavarotti and Josh Groban. Play at a slow tempo, and keep the melody angelic and lyrical.

Alexander Glazunov

(Russia, 1865–1936)

PRELUDE

(Op. 49, No. 1)

In addition to being a composer, Alexander Glazunov was also Director of the Saint-Petersburg Conservatory. Among his students was the Russian composer Dmitri Shostakovich. This lyrical work was written in 1894, and it is the first from a collection of three pieces for piano.

Peacefully

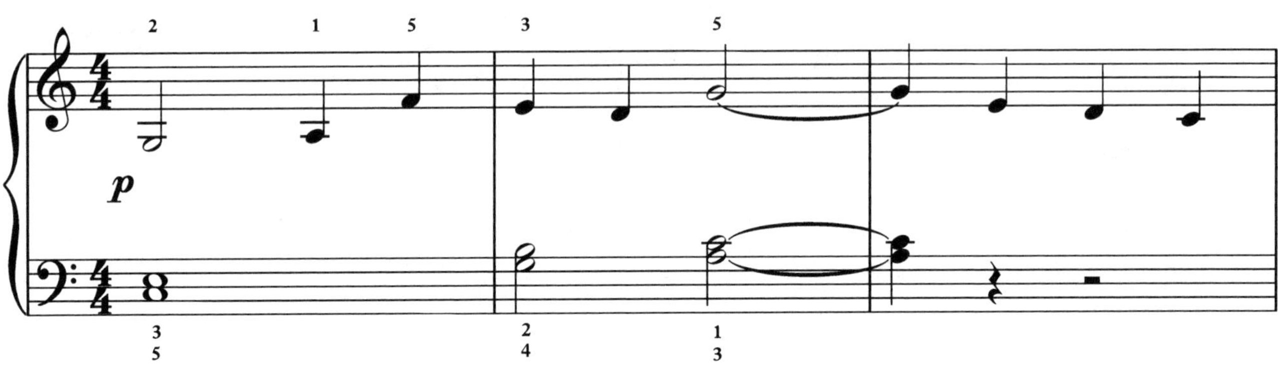

Alexander Goedicke

(Russia, 1877–1957)

Op. 6, No. 2

Alexander Goedicke was a professor at the Moscow Conservatory. He is well known for his student books, especially *Twenty Little Pieces for Beginners,* Op. 6, first published in 1902. There are passages that will require some crossing of fingers. Isolate and practice them separately. By doing so, you will optimize your practice time.

Hushed and unhurried

Alexander Goedicke

(Russia, 1877–1957)

Op. 6, No. 4

When practicing, take a close look at measures 21–27. The melodic line of the left hand crosses over into the right. Rather than having tangled fingers by trying to cross one hand into the other, you can assign certain notes to the other hand. This will keep the melody flowing smoothly, and will not interrupt the rhythm of the performance.

17
3
1
21
RH 1
LH 1
RH 1
2
LH 4
3
2
1
25
RH 1
LH 2
1
RH 1
LH 5
4
3
2
1
29
1
1
1
2
33
5
2
1
1
1
5
2
5

Alexander Goedicke

(Russia, 1877–1957)

Op. 6, No. 17

This work begins with a forceful statement of the theme. Many composers will use parallel octaves to make an announcement and highlight a melody. Both hands must play together, with no lag or hurrying between either hand. The middle section serves as contrast, and should be played softer. And once the theme returns again, it is forte.

Decisively

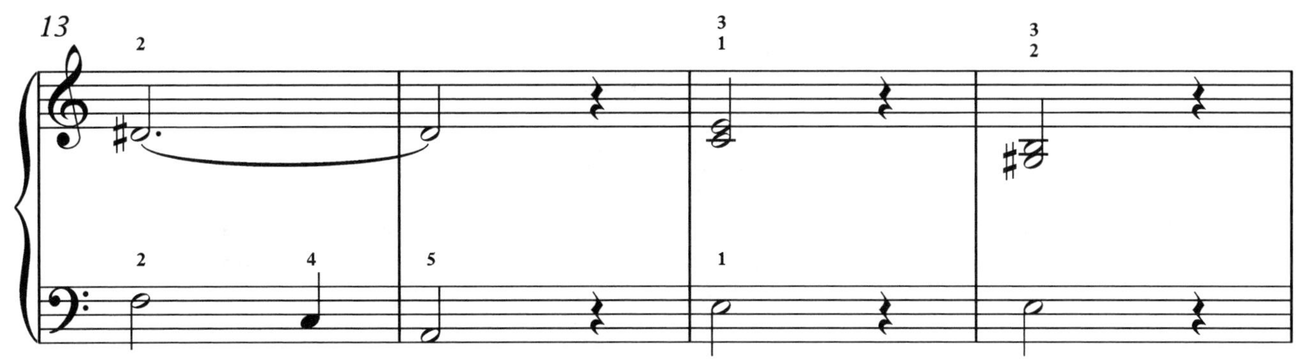
13
2
3
1
3
2
2
4
5
1

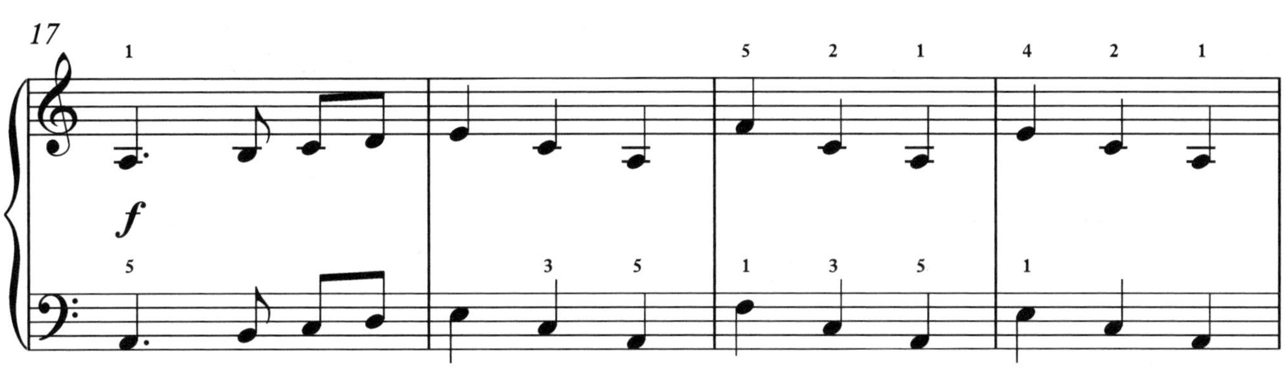
17
1
5
2
1
4
2
1
f
5
3
5
1
3
5
1

21
4
1
2
3

Alexander Goedicke

(Russia, 1877–1957)

Op. 6, No. 8

In this mournful selection, the right hand serves as a steady background to the thirds in the left. It's important to keep the tempo slow and steady, resisting the temptation to rush when notes are repeated. The left hand should fill in the sound, with a proper balance between the two musical lines.

François Joseph Gossec

(France, 1734–1829)

TAMBOURIN

Tambourin has come to be known as the composer's most famous composition, overshadowing many other of his brilliant works. It is taken from the operetta-like *Le Triomphe de la République ou le Camp de Grand Pré.* It is very characteristic of its time, and quickly became popular.

Charles Gounod

(France, 1818–1893)

Funeral Procession for a Marionette

Alfred Hitchcock popularized this work by using it as the theme music to his TV show, *Alfred Hitchcock Presents*. The work began as a satirical piece mocking a music critic, but was reworked into its present form with a narrative provided by one of Gounod's patrons. Play with a bit of mystery, and don't drag the tempo.

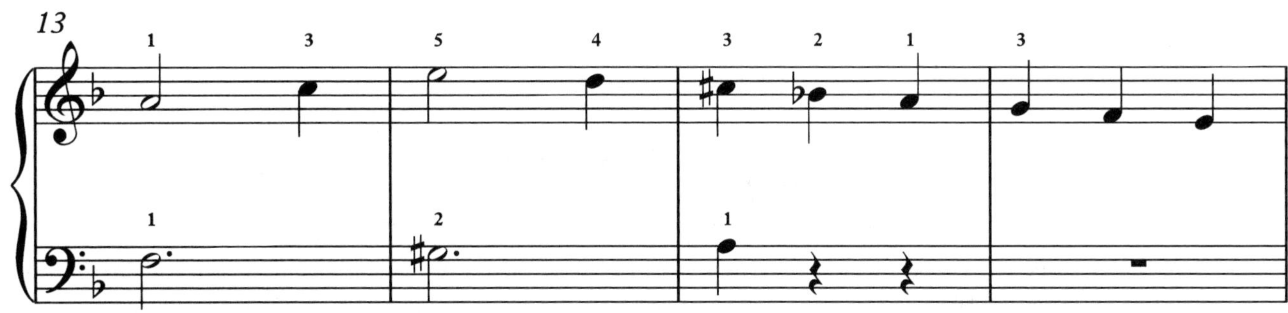
13
1
3
5
4
3
2
1
3
1
2
1

17
3
2

21
3

25
3

Edvard Grieg

(Norway, 1843–1907)

Ase's Death

(from *Peer Gynt*)

This work is taken from music Grieg wrote for the play *Peer Gynt* by Henrik Ibsen. Ase is Peer Gynt's mother, and this music accompanies her death in Scene III. Keep the mood somber while playing piano and do not rush. The steady tempo should imitate procession music.

Mournfully

Cornelius Gurlitt

(Germany, 1820–1901)

Loss

(Op. 101, No. 15)

Cornelius Gurlitt was a German composer who spent a number of years in Rome. He contributed many volumes to the repertoire of pianists, including *Album for the Young,* Op. 101. It consists of 20 characteristic pieces, expressing a variety of musical moods. When playing measure 4, use the silence of beats 3 and 4 to express the "loss" signified by the title.

Cornelius Gurlitt

(Germany, 1820–1901)

Gavotte

(Op. 117, No. 31)

The *Gavotte* is a French dance popular in the eighteenth century, characterized by steps with legs lifting up rather than the shuffling of feet. This was reminiscent of peasant dances with the music having a strong bounce. In this piece, keep that feeling present in the left hand while the melody fiddles about.

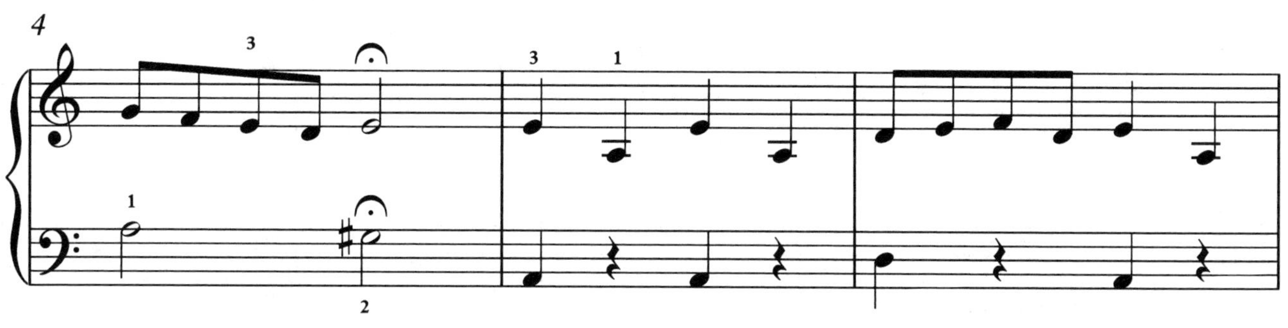

Cornelius Gurlitt

(Germany, 1820–1901)

THE POOR CHILD

(Op. 117, No. 28)

Another popular collection by Gurlitt is *First Lessons,* Op. 117. It also consists of characteristic pieces, with evocative titles that help describe the music. Be mindful of the dynamics and how they can help tell the story of the composition.

Moderato

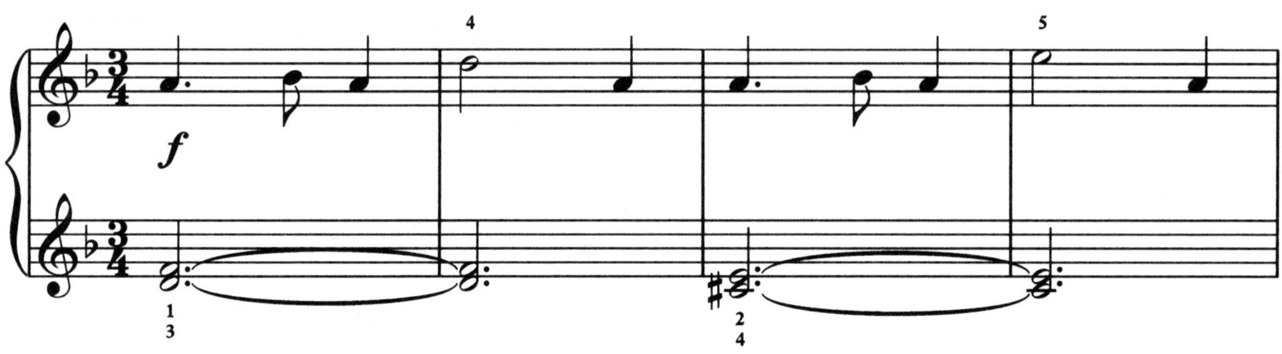

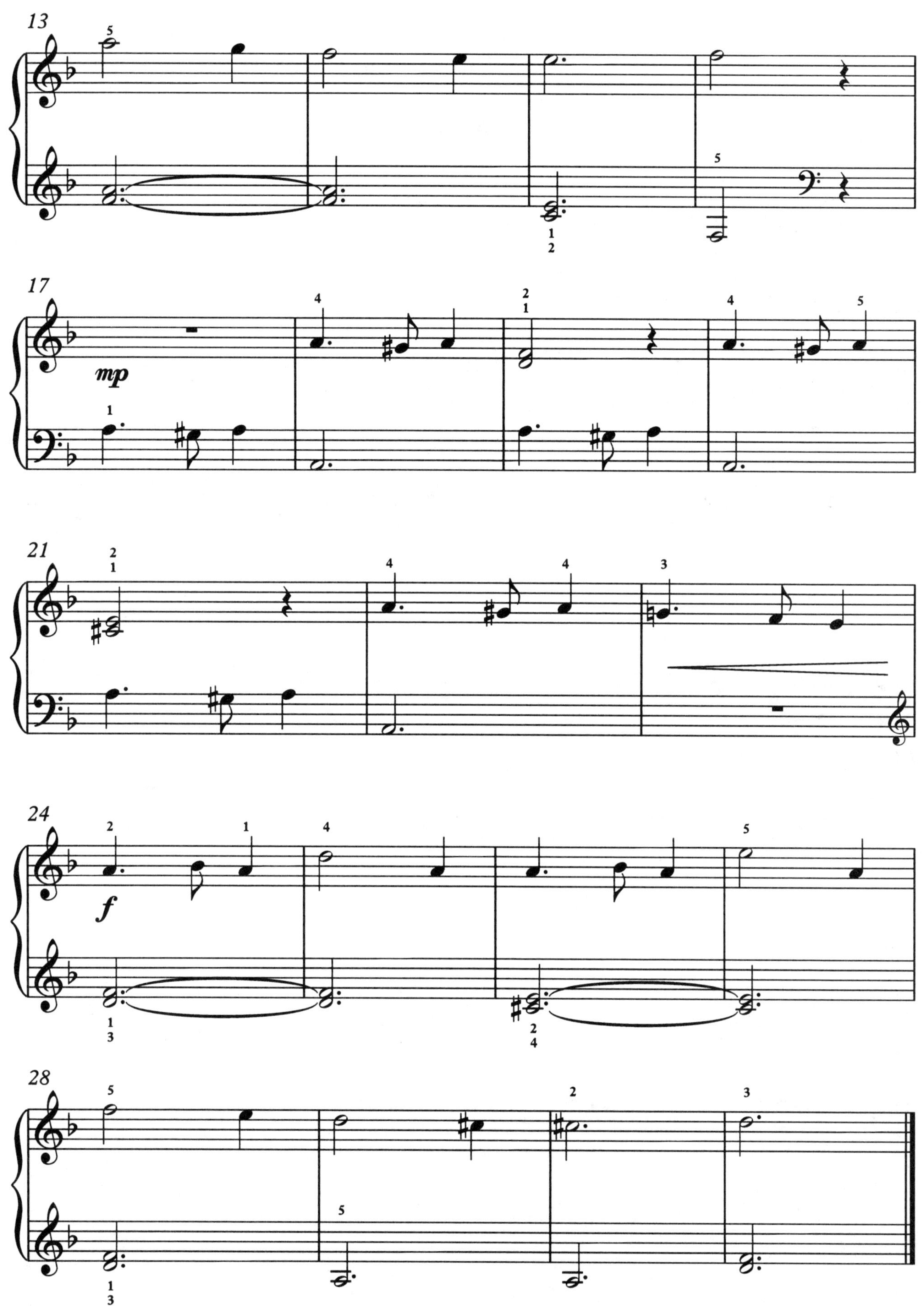

13
17
mp
21
24
f
28

Cornelius Gurlitt

(Germany, 1820–1901)

THE CLAPPERMILL

(Op. 117, No. 33)

Also from *First Lessons*, this piece should be played at a moving tempo. Both hands play phrases in one fixed position. Use the rests as a chance to reposition your hands for the next phrase.

Allegro moderato

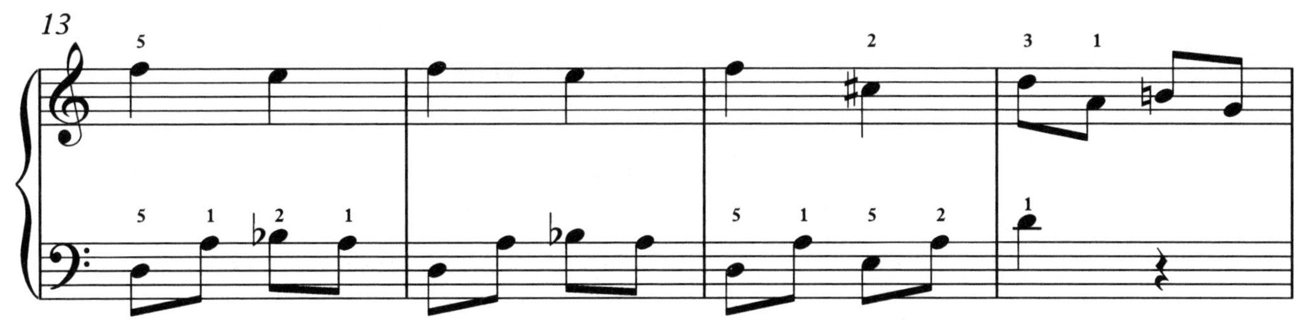
13
5
2
3
1
5
1
2
1
5
1
5
2
1

17
4
1
5
mp
2

21
4
1
2
2
1
3
mf
1

Jean Baptiste Loeillet

(Belgium, 1680–1730)

CIBEL

(Lesson III, No. 3)

Cibel is a synonym for the French dance *Gavotte* and should be played in such a manner. Dances such as these were often performed as parts of larger collections known as dance suites. Other popular dance forms were the *Sarabande, Minuet, Air,* and *Bourrée*. Each has its own steps, and it was considered quite a status symbol to have known them all.

With movement

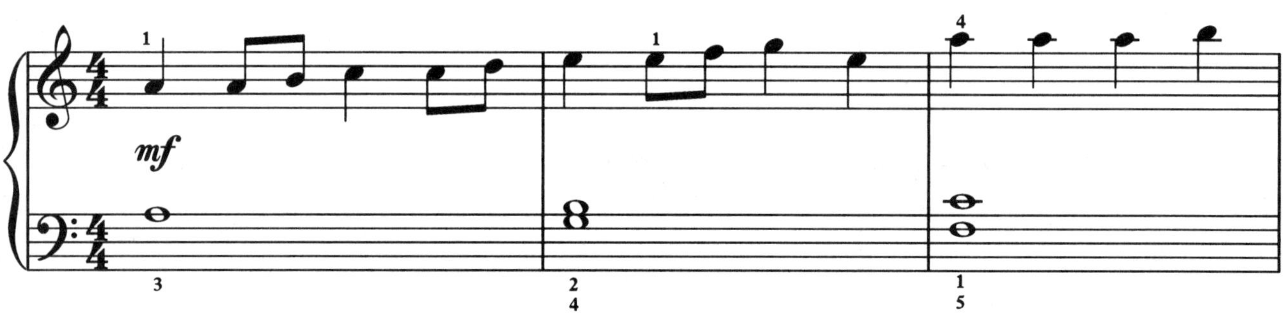

10
4
3
2
1
1
1
5
1
5

13
3
2

16
5

18
4
4
1
4
1
3
5

Gustav Mahler

(Austria 1860–1911)

Symphony No. 1

(Movement III)

Gustav Mahler was a powerful symphonist who wrote nine symphonies, and left behind sketches for a tenth. The first is nicknamed *The Titan* and contains a musical quote in the third movement. You will recognize the melody as "Frère Jacques," only sounding darker in a minor key.

Slow and heavy

Felix Mendelssohn

(Germany, 1809–1847)

Still, Still with Thee

This chorale by Felix Mendelssohn is a standard in many hymnals around the world. Harriet Beecher Stowe (author of *Uncle Tom's Cabin*) wrote the lyrics associated with it today. Play at a pace that would be comfortable for singing.

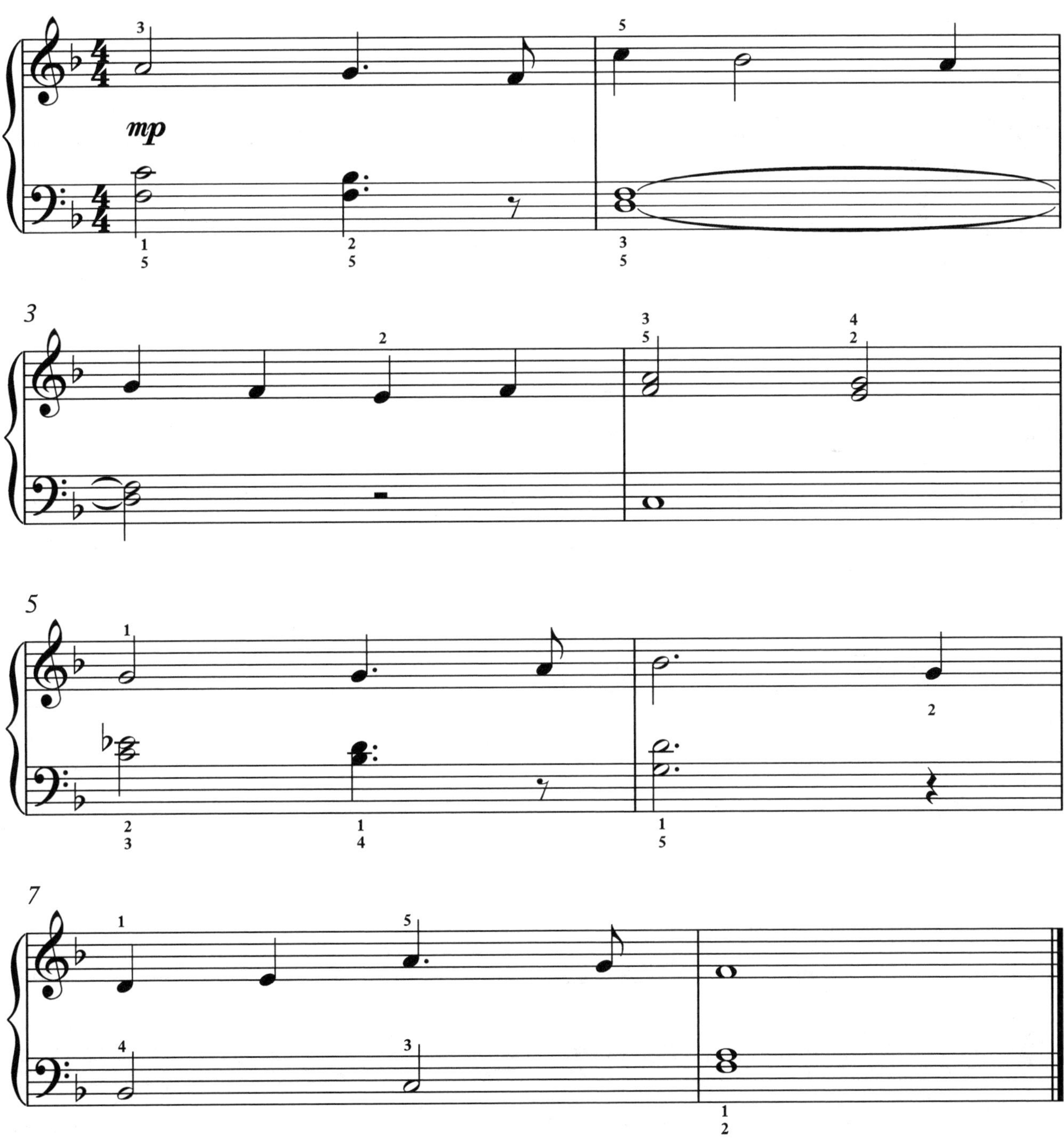

Modest Moussorgsky

(Russia, 1839–1881)

THE OLD CASTLE

(from *Pictures at an Exhibition*)

Pictures at an Exhibition is a collection of piano pieces inspired by the paintings of Viktor Hartmann, a friend of the composer's. He had recently passed away, and a large exhibition of his works was presented in Saint Petersburg. This movement was inspired by a watercolor of a medieval Italian castle. The use of open 5ths in the left hand sets an ancient tone for the melody.

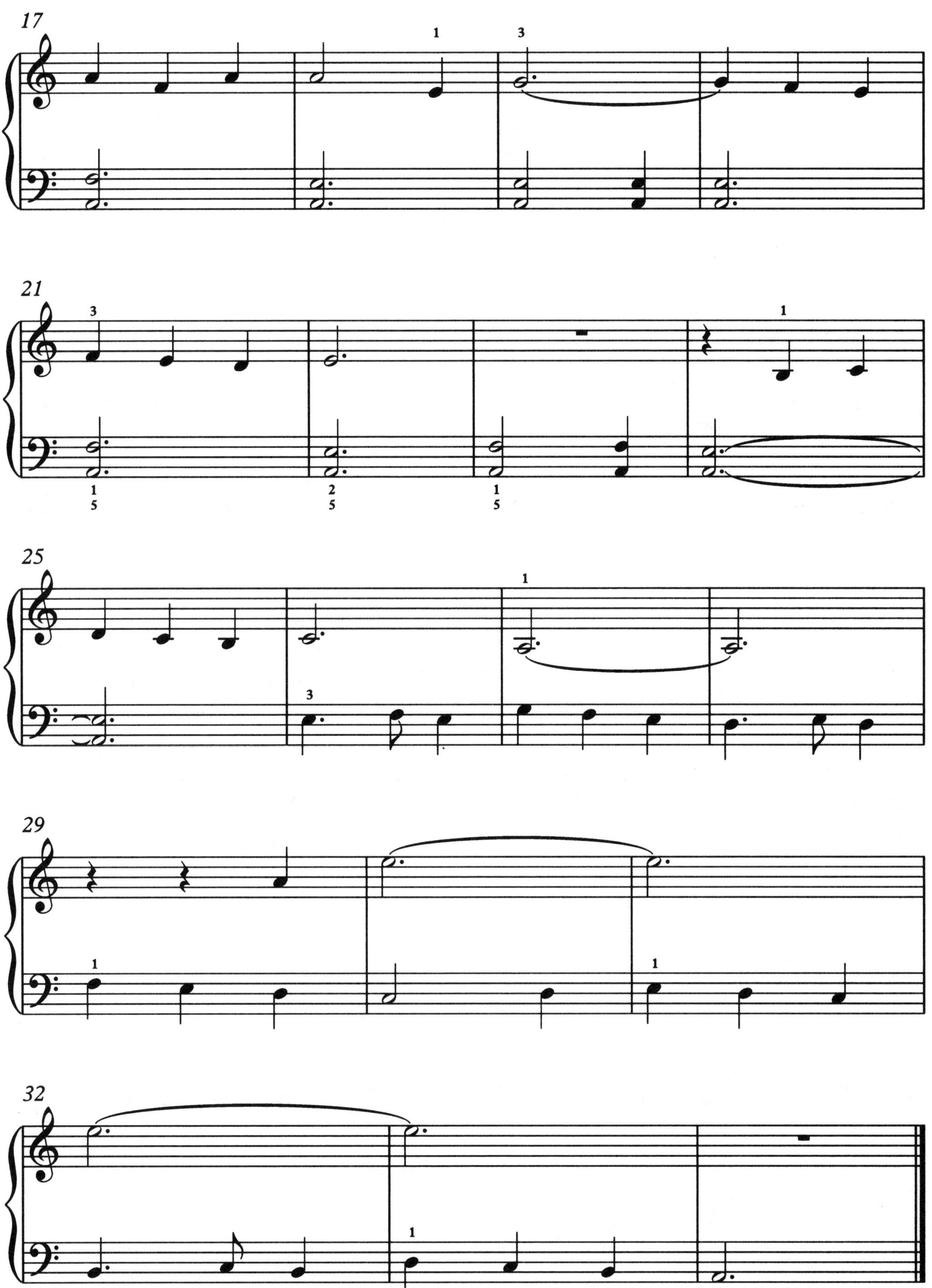
17
1
3
21
3
1
1
5
2
5
1
5
25
1
3
29
1
1
32
1

Modest Moussorgsky

(Russia, 1839–1881)

OXCART

(from *Pictures at an Exhibition*)

Oxcart is the fourth movement of the collection. It was inspired by a painting of a Polish country scene, where an ox is toiling with a cart on large wheels. The music aptly interprets the scene, using a heavy repeated bass line to pull along the melody.

Slow and heavy

10
13
16
19
22

Wolfgang Amadeus Mozart

(Austria, 1756–1791)

Exultate Jubilate, K. 165

This solo motet was composed in 1773 when Mozart was sixteen. It is one of his better known religious works and is frequently performed in concert settings. The F# in measure 4 is characteristic of Mozart's style. Use it to lean into the next note—G.

Moderato

Jacques Offenbach

(Germany, 1819–1880)

Can Can

The *cancan* was a popular French dance in the 1840s that featured high kicks and splits. Offenbach included it in his operetta *Orpheus in the Underworld,* known in the story as the "Galop Infernal." It has since become a familiar tune around the world.

Johann Pachelbel

(Germany, 1653–1706)

FUGA

A *fuga* (or fugue) is a musical form based on a short theme known as a subject. The subject is stated by each voice and serves as the main material as the music develops. In this two-voice fuga, the subject of the first movement appears in both hands and is repeated.

7
1
3
4
5
4
3

9
3
1
1
2

11
5

13

Henry Purcell

(England, 1659–1695)

Air in E Minor

Henry Purcell was a highly celebrated English Baroque composer. His works defined a British style, unique from those that were developing in other countries. He became the organist and composer-in-residence at Westminster Abbey, where he was honored by being buried adjacent to the organ there. Purcell was celebrated during his lifetime, and is still highly revered to this day.

Moderato

Albert Pieczonka

(Russia, 1828–1912)

TARANTELLA

Albert Pieczonka is a lesser-known composer who emigrated to the United States in 1880. His most famous work is this *Tarantella*. The lively dance form in triple meter originated in the Taranto region of Italy. Practice the work slowly at first, then solidly build up to a quicker tempo.

Tarantella

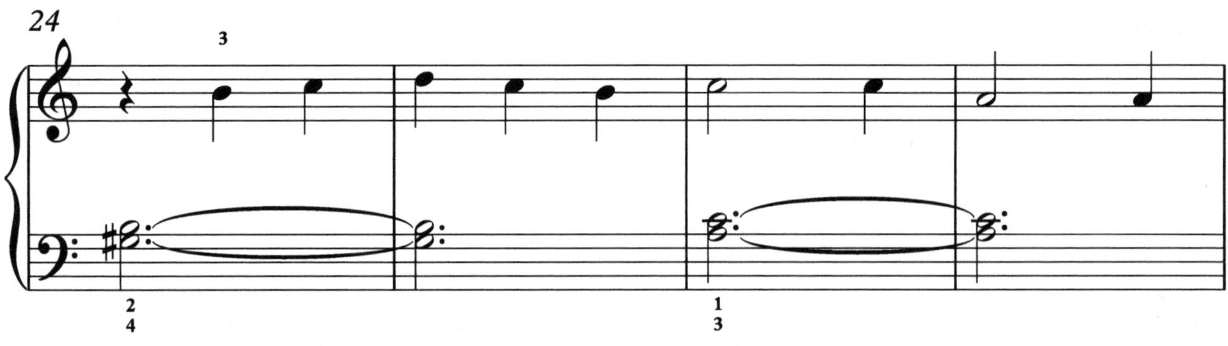

32
1
5
2

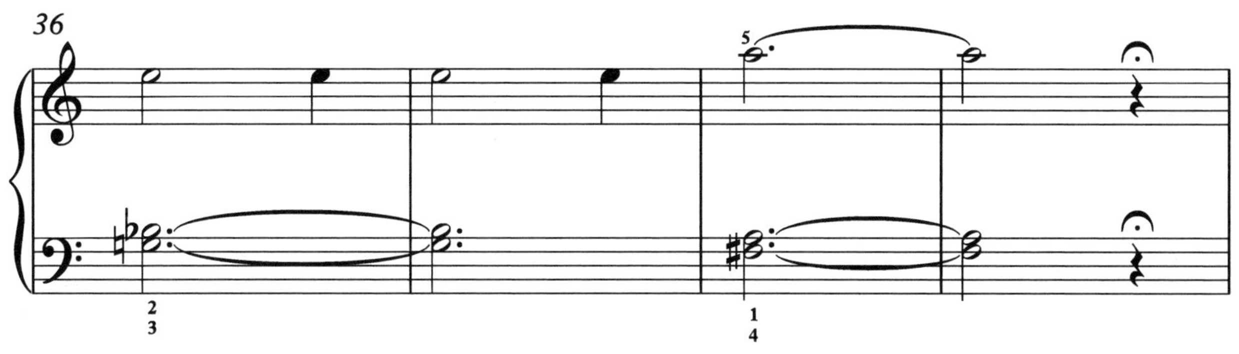
36
5
2
3
1
4

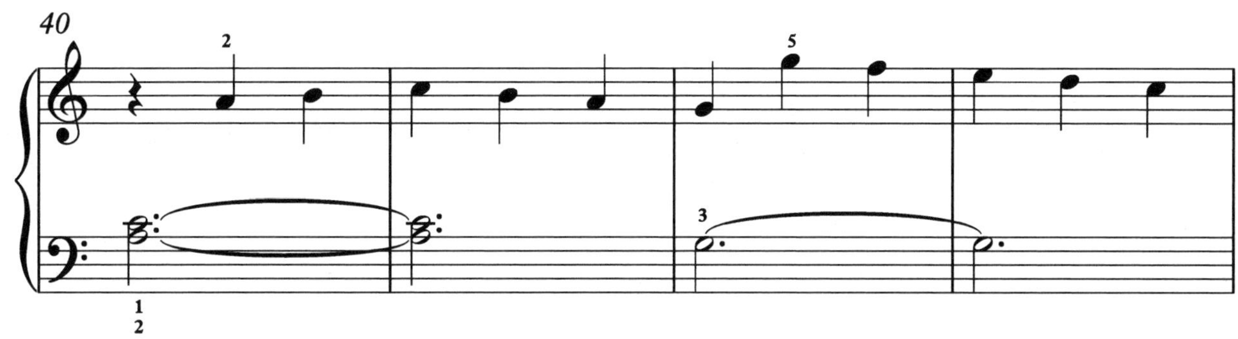
40
2
5
3
1
2

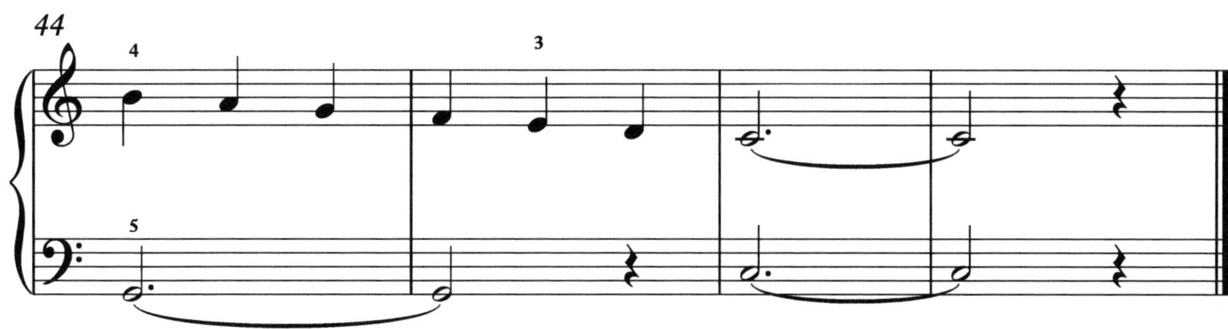
44
4
3
5

Sergei Rachmaninoff

(Russia, 1873–1943)

Ave Maria

(from *All-Night Vigil,* Op. 37)

This *Ave Maria* is from one of Rachmaninoff's most celebrated works. It is also one of his own favorite personal compositions. As is customary in the Russian Orthodox Church, the original is sung *a cappella* (without instruments). Phrase as if you were singing along.

Jean-Philippe Rameau

(France, 1683–1764)

La Boiteuse

(from *Pièces de Clavecin*)

Jean-Philippe Rameau was a composer and music theorist. His *Treatise on Harmony* (1722) helped define modern music theory, especially how we understand chords. This work is from a larger collection known as *Pièces de Clavecin* (1724), and is the last of ten movements.

Jean-Philippe Rameau

(France, 1683–1764)

CYCLOPS

(from *Pièces de Clavecin*)

Also from *Pièces de Clavecin*, this is the eighth movement. The opening should be played confidently and with a big sound. This piece demonstrates why scales and arpeggios are important to practice. In measures 5 and 9, one note is played by different thumbs as the music moves from the left to the right hand.

Allegro moderato

Jean-Philippe Rameau

(France, 1683–1764)

Minuet

(from *Pièces de clavecin avec une méthode*)

This minuet is one of Rameau's most popular works. It is the first piece in another, similarly named collection, *Pièces de clavecin avec une méthode.* Minuets were part of the dance suites popular in this era, and they are in three-four time. Use the pause at the fermata as a chance to reset your hands (and wrists) in the next position.

Allegretto

Anton Rubinstein

(Russia, 1829–1894)

Kameni Ostrov, No. 8

Anton Rubinstein was an accomplished pianist, composer, and conductor. He is also remembered as the founder of the St. Petersburg Conservatory. While there, he was Tchaikovsky's composition teacher. This work is the eighth in the collection *Kameni Ostrov* ("Stone Island").

Moderato

Anton Rubinstein

(Russia, 1829–1894)

Kameni Ostrov, No. 22

The repeated pattern in the right hand is an effect known as *ostinato*. Play evenly, and use the eighth notes to keep time. The notes slightly change at measure 9, so do not lose concentration just because the pattern is repeated. Also, be sure the right hand does not overpower the lyrical melody in the left.

Gentle and unhurried

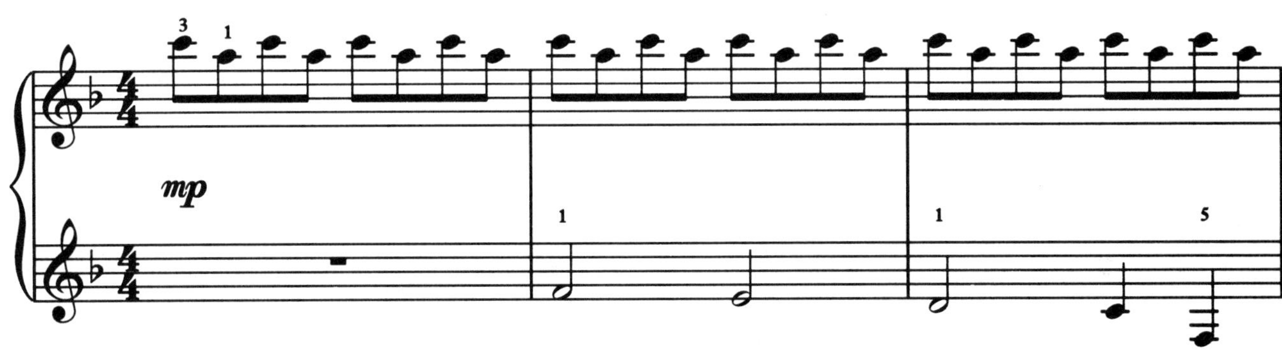

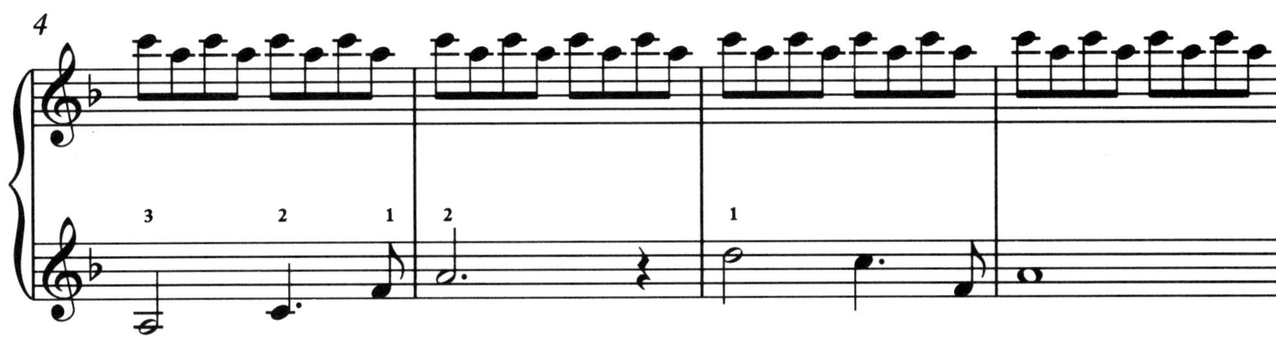

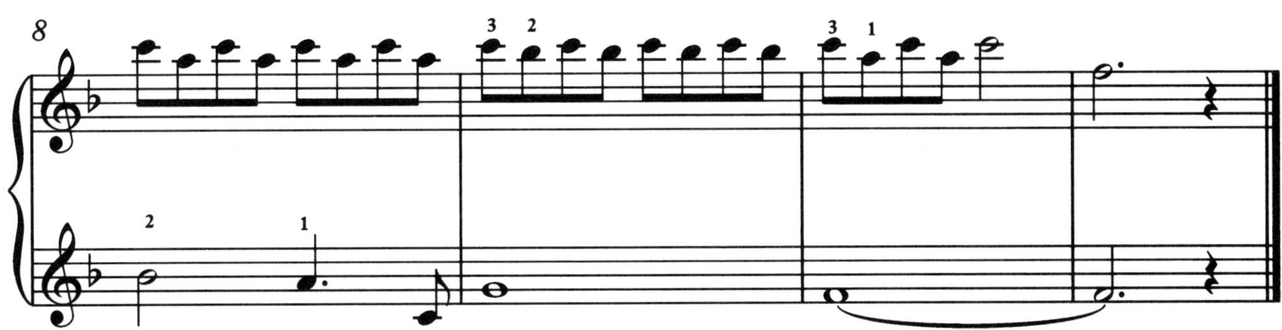

Anton Rubinstein

(Russia, 1829–1894)

ROMANCE

(Op. 44, No. 1)

This is the first movement of *6 Soirées à Saint-Petersbourg*. Be mindful of the sharps in the beginning. In measure 1, the C# serves as a passing tone between C and D. In measures 2 and 3, the D# is a lower neighbor. It helps give the E melodic emphasis.

With feeling

Camille Saint-Saëns

(France, 1835–1921)

Elephant

(from *Carnival of the Animals*)

Carnival of the Animals is a fourteen-movement work, each depicting a different animal. The animals include kangaroos, tortoises, birds, and, in the fifth movement, an elephant. By having the melody played low in the left hand, a musical image of a hefty animal is created.

Erik Satie

(France, 1866–1925)

Je Te Veux

The title of this popular love song means "I Want You" in French. Satie used a text by Henry Pacory, and it was written for a singer whom Satie had been accompanying. The poem was a bit racy for its time, which only added to the popularity of the song. Revel in the rich harmonies that Satie uses to interpret the poem.

Franz Schubert

(Austria, 1797–1828)

Valse Noble

(Op. 77, No. 1)

This is the first of the *12 Valses Nobles* ("12 Noble Waltzes") written in 1827, one year before Schubert's death. They are colorful miniatures that helped elevate the waltz as a form suitable for solo piano.

Franz Schubert

(Austria, 1797–1828)

Cradle Song

(Op, 98, No. 2)

This beautiful lullaby has become one of Schubert's most performed works. It is also commonly known by its German title, *Wiegenlied*. Perform it in a gentle and soothing manner.

Peter Ilyitch Tchaikovsky

(Russia, 1840–1893)

SYMPHONY NO. 4

(Movement II)

Tchaikovsky's six symphonies are famous and have become orchestral standards. The fourth is nicknamed "Fate," and was dedicated "To My Best Friend," which was revealed to be his patroness Madame von Meck. This long, thematic line should be played gracefully, using the fermata as a chance to breathe. In the original, it is played by an oboe.

10

13

16

19

Peter Ilyitch Tchaikovsky

(Russia, 1840–1893)

Symphony No. 4

(Movement IV)

Symphony No. 4 uses a Russian folk-song as the basis for the fourth movement. The name of the song is "Beriozka" ("The White Birch") and should be played with an upbeat tempo.

Georg Philipp Telemann

(Germany, 1681–1767)

Gavotte in C Major

Georg Philipp Telemann was a very busy Baroque composer, with more than 800 surviving works. The *Guinness Book of World Records* lists him as the most prolific composers of all time. He was celebrated during his lifetime and was close friends with Johann Sebastian Bach, who asked him to be the godfather of his son Carl Philipp Emanuel.

Georg Philipp Telemann

(Germany, 1681–1767)

Gavotte in A Minor

This second gavotte by Telemann is in A minor, but ends in C major. A minor is related to C major, and is known as its relative minor key. The sixth scale degree is always the relative minor of any major key. For example: G major's relative minor is E, and F major's relative minor is D minor. You can hear the difference in color between the two keys in this work.

Richard Wagner

(Germany, 1813–1883)

Siegfried Idyll

This is the opening of a famous tone poem by Richard Wagner. It was written for his wife as a birthday gift, and its first performance was a surprise. On Christmas morning, musicians quietly assembled in Wagner's home at the bottom of his staircase. His wife, Cosima, awoke to the beautiful music.

Johann Georg Witthauer

(Germany, 1750–1802)

GAVOTTE

Johann Georg Witthauer was a German composer who studied with C. P. E. Bach. This popular work was written circa 1786 and published in a larger collection. Bring out the left-hand lines in measures 3 and 6, and use the G# in the next measure to emphasize the A. This is an opportunity for the left hand to be expressive.

Duets

Traditional

CHOPSTICKS

Piano II

Traditional

CHOPSTICKS

Piano I

Johann Sebastian Bach

(Germany, 1685–1750)

CHORALE NO. 96

("Jesu, Meine Freude")

Piano II

Steady

5

9

Johann Sebastian Bach

(Germany, 1685–1750)

CHORALE NO. 96

("Jesu, Meine Freude")

Piano I

Steady

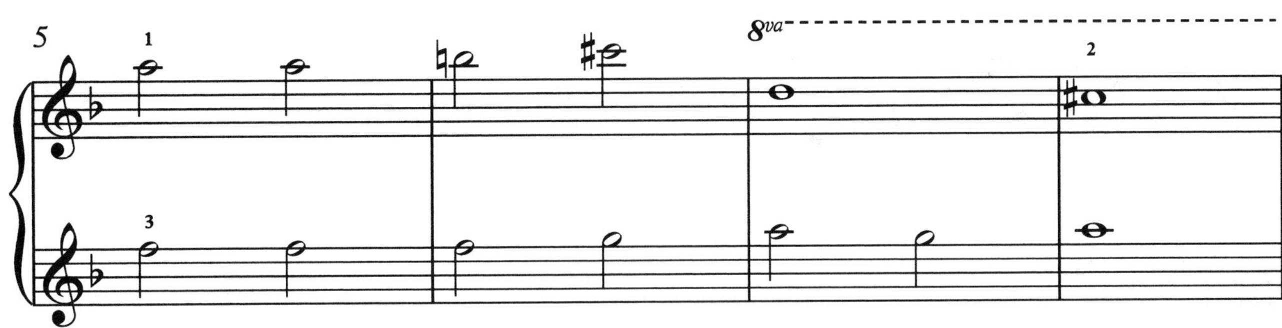

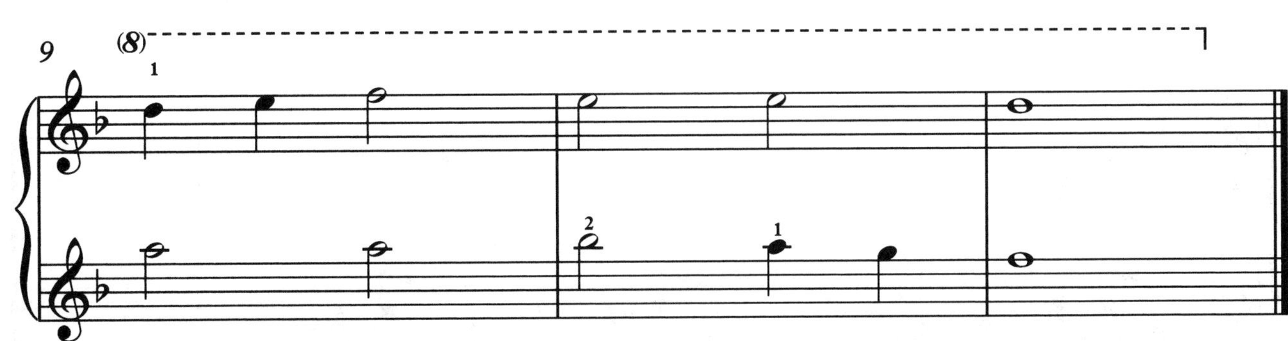

Ludwig van Beethoven

(Germany, 1770–1827)

Für Elise

Piano II

Ludwig van Beethoven

(Germany, 1770–1827)

FÜR ELISE

Piano I

Modest Moussorgsky

(Russia, 1839–1881)

Great Gates of Kiev

(from *Pictures at an Exhibition*)

Piano II

Modest Moussorgsky

(Russia, 1839–1881)

GREAT GATES OF KIEV

(from *Pictures at an Exhibition*)

Piano I

Wolfgang Amadeus Mozart

(Austria, 1756–1791)

SYMPHONY NO. 25

(Movement I)

Piano II

Allegro con brio

Wolfgang Amadeus Mozart

(Austria, 1756–1791)

SYMPHONY NO. 25

(Movement I)

Piano I

NOTES

NOTES

NOTES

NOTES

NOTES